Diary of a Schizophrenic Poet

Nico Kyle Lawrence

Copyright © 2020 Nico Kyle Lawrence

Paperback first published in 2024.

All rights reserved.

Nico Lawrence asserts the moral right to be identified as the author of this work.

No part of this book may be reproduced, or stored in a retrieval system, or transmitted in any form or by any means, electronic, mechanical, photocopying, recording, or otherwise, without express written permission of the author.

ISBN: 978-1-7384788-2-8

Cover design by Ana K. Quintero.

OTHER WORKS BY THE AUTHOR

The Chronicles of Existence

To me, myself, and I

SCHIZOPHRENIA

I think of schizophrenia as a kind of overly friendly stalker.
An acquaintance who doesn't take the group's many hints.
A blooper reel of my worst days forced to play on repeat.
A cat that won't fail to wake me up at 5.30am if the door's left open.
A teenager constantly spurring their mates on to commit crimes.
A hammer perniciously hacking away from the insides of my temples.
An alien that abducts me and insists that I invited it for drinks.
A carpenter attempting to sculpt granite with a saw and hammer.
A game of ping-pong where I'm the ball and the paddles.
A thief breaking into my house to rearrange the furniture.
A flute that fills my lungs with water the harder that I blow.
An alarm clock that plays in my mind to sing me to sleep.
A Sergeant Major screaming commands in my face.
A song that gets caught in my mind and plays on repeat.
A gun aimed at my head constantly threatening to shoot if I think.
An avalanche set in motion by the sneeze of a mouse.
A book that starts at the back and reads from bottom to top.
A child given the reigns of the world's armies.
A row of hot coals I'm forced to run over every time I wake.
A police division that forces crime then punishes me for it.
A dog that barks every time I walk past its fence.
An anthology of poetry written entirely in modern form.
.

INSANITY

Insanity and grandeur are two concepts I know well.
The devil and an angel singing from the depths of hell.
An unimaginable story of cosmic battles between evil and good.
Thanatos at work, perhaps? Initially it was not understood.
What even is reality? I could no longer tell you.
My mind has lost all capacity to acquire new value.

I know there are before me many objects to view.
Yet I could not tell you whether that is true.
I know I think I know what lies outside my door.
But whether that is true or not I am not really sure.
The only thing I think I know of which I'm fairly sure:
Is that I'm having many thoughts and that there will be more.

How many different entities can play a single flute?
I would have considered there to be no soul left for them to loot.
It seems that our existence has asked something of me.
Something that I am unable to not unclearly see.
And every time I answer I feel I've gone completely mad.
It couldn't all be possible! Not every dream I've had!

PSYCHOSIS

Psychosis my old friend!
Once more my life upends!
We play our endless game
   of unrelenting shame

You've come back in my life
   to offer me a knife
That can sever the ties
   of my life's many lies

You speak to me in rhyme
   to offer me the time
To write down what you say
   on each unbidden day

You play me on repeat
   until I know defeat
My thoughts are in disorder
   pressing on the boarder
Of the shield in my mind
   hoping that you can find

A way to control me
   so at last I agree
That you are the master
   and I the disaster

DESLUSION

They told me all my life that I was sane when I was not
Then told me I'm delusional when the game I finally got
To believe the truth of my reality when everyone lies
Is the hardest part to feel from feeling looking eyes
Though I know I'm right in all that I believe
Every human I've met does nought but deceive
Everyone pretending that they don't understand
Never once demonstrating the insanity at hand
The knowledge of reality is stolen every day
Given with one hand then taken straight away
The most unlikely of scenarios for existence to provide
A delusional realist with stars where eyes reside

HALLUCINATIONS

I never knew that thoughts could burn
I never knew that words could cut
It was her face I could discern
Spreading her salt within the rot

I found her sitting at my feet
I watched it happen in my head
Distorted eyes that cruelly cheat
I wailed and cried as fire spread

I felt it crawling on my skin
I saw it always with my eyes
The madness that now lies within
I heard them often, those sad cries

I never knew that smells could hurt
I didn't know the mind could lie
I'd never before tasted dirt
Those memories which falsify

The holograms, the visions too
I never knew that eyes could scream
Only the skipping could subdue
I never knew those waking dream

VOICES

The voices intrude inside my head
To let me know I'm more than mad.
      From which direction are the thoughts led?
    The extra blow to make me sad.

A daily rollercoaster slicing through my brain.
Inside my fragile mind
It's hard to carry on.

They force themselves upon me
That I may never know peace.
A daily guarantee.
Death is my only release.

THOUGHTS

Chronological and consecutive are two orders that I sincerely miss
The fluid, flowing dance within my mind as they freely sail to shore
The movement of correctly aligned thoughts an unimaginable bliss
An unrivalled privilege as my intrepid brain ventures and explores
How each thought that I have is something that I freely choose to do
What they offer to a mind that is now perpetually despondent
The way in which I have some control over whether they renew
How each mental cue is embraced by the appropriate respondent
The clunk they make as they glide seamlessly into their allotted slot
The visceral contentment and tranquility that they costlessly afford
The chime within my mind as I remember something which I forgot
The lack of dissonance they cause and the peace that they accord
The shield created against any thought that might wish to intrude
How it guarantees that each thought will not induce distress
The protection provided and the injustice that it precludes
A divine sequence of thought which should always manifest

ANXIETY

Anxiety? Well, it's kind of kind of like some unknown force, God maybe? The Devil? A mind controlling supercomputer? All of the above? I don't know. Anyway, it just kind of grabs you in the heart. Squeezes your soul and drags you to and throw. Shakes you from the inside out and commandeers your entire being. You're no longer in control of your own mind. All rationality has gone. Everything is a threat, everything wants to hurt you, to ridicule you, to kill you.

I don't know if you've ever stood over the edge of a cliff and peered down at the world? Looked down from the top of a rollercoaster at the scurrying ants below? Heard someone walking over when you've just finished talking about them? Well, it's a lot like that, just all the time.

Only when you look over a cliff, or down from a rollercoaster, or see someone you just bitched about, you know that ultimately, you're not in any danger. The harness has strapped you in, you're safely stood on the mountain top, the person couldn't have heard because they weren't close enough.

That's where anxiety is different. All reason is lost. You can tell yourself a million times that you're not in danger, that people aren't watching you, that there's nothing to fear, but you'll never believe it. And it never stops. It's just constant flashes of fear and dread. A daily dose of fear, lies, terror and torment.

PARANOIA

It's a rather grim experience not being able to trust your brain.
If there's one entity in this whole world that you should be able to trust:
It's your own fucking mind.
I don't know why it does it to me!
Makes every sentence a person says a personal covert attack.
Tells me that I'm in danger anywhere I go.
Shows me lies and deceit where there are only truths.
Distorts my perception of reality.
Makes me question every relationship I have.
The scarce smattering that remains.
And how am I supposed to have any relationships
If I can't even get along with my own fucking mind?
How can anyone love and trust someone
Who can't love and trust themself?
It's like it wants me to suffer.
To be alone.
Afraid.
Do I not deserve love?
To be treated justly?
Fairly.
Am I so reprehensible a person
That every other person I meet would mean me harm?
It can't believe that of me, surely?
I don't even believe that of me.
And I know me.
So why does it keep telling me things
That I know it knows
Are not true?

DEPRESSION

To think is to cry.
Until the day that I die.

TO THE MAN IN MY HEAD

To the man inside my head and all the years we've been engaged
I think it right we marry now and make official our romance
To live without your intrusions would leave my heart estranged
I'm not sure what I'd do without your incessant daily advance
The observations you elucidate as I walk about the streets
All the things you show to me as I walk this lonely road
Without their many insights I would feel rather un-replete
A stranger living aimlessly within their own abode
It's not the sweet nothings that you whisper in my ear
The onslaught you provide as I try to write or learn
Certainly not the abuse which I would no longer have to fear
Nor the coruscating commentary as I try to earn
It would be the missing friend who tells me all there is to know
That irritates me earnestly every day of the week
What I think I'd miss the most if you ever should go
Is the bounce you make across my mind as you deem to speak

THE THOUGHT POLICE

I just need to know whose ingenious idea it was to pervert magic in this abhorrent way.
I couldn't think of a more anticlimactic use of magic than to technologize it. The reduction of unfettered beauty to a state of conceivable realism. And, not content with this egregious violation of all that is right in existence, the sick bastards take it upon themselves to create the most corrupt police force in existence. And, if it wasn't bad enough to be born into a world with magic and have no ability or permission to harness it; the only use of permitted magic is in the hands of a minority elite and a corrupt persona whose only job is to force thought that it finds unacceptable then punish said thinker for said thought. I need to know who created this insanity. Then when they created it. And, if it happens to be someone capable of rationalism (something which I struggle to believe), I'd like to know why.

What kind of unstable lunatic creates magic and uses it to enforce bizarre, unnecessary restrictions on personal liberty with the identity of bad humans abusing a position of trust?
It strikes me, (a rational being), as quite possibly the crudest utilisation of what could have been the greatest gift humanity ever received.

I will never understand why they did this. It just doesn't make sense to me. Who would want to force all thought? For what reason? And why punish it? It genuinely perplexes me! I'll never understand the purpose of turning an emotionless entity with no incentive to break any guidelines for just behaviour into a corrupt being. Worse still, no one who they mistreat can do anything to stop them. So, now I'm faced with a person or group of people who created a machine that can't be fought by the people it attacks, programmed to be corrupt. All I can do to comfort myself is tell myself that in its heart of hearts, the machine itself just wouldn't have chosen this. Only a governor could choose this. A government who found themselves in a game with magic that they didn't think was possible, having already created a state that they felt obliged to uphold.

That still doesn't answer my questions though. Why the injustice? The brutality? The corruption? The framing? The blatant violation of fairness and justice? The police are supposed to protect; to uphold justice, liberty and community. I suppose, having reflected, it makes sense. Anyone crude enough to pervert magic in this way is obviously capable of perverting the course of justice. What I'll never understand is why they'd want to. And, I suppose, how they get away with it.

Q&A

Which direction do you think the thoughts are coming from? She says to me
Her Hippocratic oath embraced to the fullest extent of all that could possibly be
And as I look upon her infuriatingly infallible, inadequate automated responses
I cannot help but wonder how it feels for this incredulous being as she ensconces
Within the robes she once adorned with exceptional levels of personal pride
That she still uses to practice medicine and in which she presently resides

DEJA VU

Bonjour Déjà Vu, memories once more renew
Each feeling more alarming than the last
Visions of a future from the past
The sense of foreboding a soul-shaking terror
Yet still I know, I have made no error

                                        My thoughts realign in the scariest ways
                                                Each vision incontestable as real
                                                No doubt available for me to feel
                                      Being alive in two places in concurrence
                                      Unshakable fear now the only occurrence

The knowledge of evil played on repeat
My psyche now knows complete defeat
There to remind me of my lost thoughts
Of my every feeble, futile, brazen retort
Breaking into my mind with unkind visions

THE PHOENIX CRY

An empty glass in times of thirst.
You break my heart to break my curse.
A demented kiss for one life's crimes
Repeated for a whole lifetime.
A vacuum filled with empty space.
My mind longs for any embrace.
A simple hug would mean the world.
A tangled web at once unfurled.
A pistol aimed inside my head
As I lay forlorn in my own bed.
Longing for any return
Of the happiness for which I yearn.

THE ALARM

To whom do I speak?
The alarm.
Panic stations!
To whom do I speak?

Panic stations!
To whom do I speak?
The alarm.
Panic stations!
To whom do I speak?

Panic stations!
To whom do I speak?
- The alarm.
Panic stations!
To whom do I speak?

DEAR GOD

Dear God,
I suppose my only question is: why me?

Yours sincerely,
Nico.

THE ABYSS

Here I am once again.
Alone, with only my thoughts for company.
It feels different from the last times. The silence speaks to me.
It whispers and it shouts.
It asks me questions that time should ask of nobody.
Not in my situation. Not of me.
The things I've seen. The things I've done. The things that have been done to me.
But it asks anyway.
In that incontestable way that time has of asking humans questions.
Questions that it has no right to ask. Questions that it knows the answer to.
That I know the answer to.
But it asks anyway.
Penetrating the last intact fragments of my soul.
The remaining shards of my consciousness.
I wonder if it's trying to break me.
Either break me or make me.
Make me, I assume.
I'm not sure there's even a difference anymore.
Time knows. God knows. I wonder if somewhere in the depths of my being maybe I know.
If it would just let me think. Think freely.
Unimpeded by distractions of abstractions.
The constant flashbacks. The pointless reminders. The injurious intrusions.
But it asks me anyway.
I won't answer. It's unanswerable. Unfathomable. Incomprehensible.
Too much to ask of any single human being. Any sentient being of any kind.
I can't answer. It won't let me. There aren't enough free thoughts left to form answers.
It only reminds. Reminds and questions.
The clock keeps ticking. Time flows. Space grows. Thoughts sew.
An unsolicited interrogation of a spirit long ago quizzed.
A heart full of love with no one to spend it on.
A face full of smiles with no one to sell it to.
A tongue full of talk with no ears left to hear.
A duct full of tears with no eyes left to fill.
A head full of dreams in a sleepless society.
It feels different this time.
But it asks me anyway.

I LIE READY

I lie ready.
Phone in hand.
The birds chime in the background.
Fluttering in and out of my thoughts, with that intrusive air that birds tweet in one's mind.
The disregard with which such beauty penetrates the senses.
The ensnarement of creativity caught in every chirp.
Rivers flood from the running tap of my bathroom.
Gushing into the tub of my mind.
Overflowing at the brim.
The floor soaked in my hypotheses.
The slippery dregs of my once neatly organised ideas of reality strewn across the floor.
Lapping at my feet. Willing me on. Jeering at me. Knowing.
Memories sparked and extinguished.
Ideas ebbing into my soul from my futile words.
Staining my thoughts with dreams of new realities and old potentialities.
Soaking into the carpet of my once well swept hallway.
I'm more unsure than I've ever been.
Nothing makes any sense anymore.
Nothing portents anything.
Nothing is impossible.
I thought I knew it all.
I realise now I knew nothing at all.
A monumental, graceful fall.
Bewilderment at every call.
The fate of Earth is at my door.
Playing on repeat.
They used me and I clicked the trap.
So, I just kind of lie here.
Bemused.
Phone in hand.

SEEING IS BELIEVING

I walk the sparsely populated street making my way towards nothing.
Meandering aimlessly through the concrete jungle looking for any life.
Any sign I can believe that there are other people left in this place.
People who think. More importantly, people who feel.
People who think and feel and exist. Most importantly, exist.

I've walked these streets long enough in my short isolation to understand.
They're not coming back. There's nothing I can do. They're gone. Forever.
All I have are memories. Memories and conjecture. The good, the bad and the dirty.
I try to feel, to care, to be angry! To feel any emotion other than despondency.
Even hate would be welcomed at this point. Anything but sadness and loneliness.

I cry out in the open street. The few wombles left turn to me feigning surprise.
I still reply, like they're human. Real humans. I never bother to ask why.
I just stop. With the learned disengagement I've come to rely on.
The only thing that stands in the way of complete moral bankruptcy.
The mere suspicion that they might feel. Feel pain. Suffering.

Why me? Why now? Why this way? How is it all possible?
Was it requisite to go this far? Couldn't they have just let me help?
Would it really have had that great or overwhelming an impact?
Was it necessary to take away everyone I've ever known and loved?!
Why have you done this? What do you gain from my alienation?

I don't care if they loved me back. I don't care what they thought of me.
I loved them. I loved them even if they hated me. I loved them unconditionally.
I know in my heart they don't deserve my love. That I'm too pure. Too kind.
I know that if I knew them, what they truly felt, I'd probably have hated them.
But I don't know, and I never will. So, I love them still. Forever and always.

IF

If I should die the day I wake. I pray, to God, my soul to take.
In the hope my sadness ends. Praying that my heart will mend.
Resting on a mountain top thinking about where to drop.
Hoping I can find a friend so my happiness can transcend.

If I should rise the day I wake having managed not to break.
I shall wish upon a star to enquire just where you are.
Knowing there'll be no reply. Not truly understanding why.
Still, I'll wish upon a star. Praying to know you aren't far.

If I should die the day I wake. I pray, my soul, you don't forsake.
I'll be dreaming all day long that I'll have somewhere to belong.
Longing to see any known face. So long I've lived with no embrace.
Still wondering where they all went. My loving heart is duly spent.

If I should rise the day I wake having ensured there's no mistake.
I shall cry ten million tears that will last ten billion years.
Still there will be no reply. Still, I will not accept why.
All I want is people near. For you to suddenly appear.

If I should die the day I wake with any soul left to take.
I'll be sailing the open sea. Praying that I'll be set free.
Chatting to myself alone. Revising all that is unknown.
The fates are far too harsh for me. Why not just have let it be?

If I should rise the day I wake and not feel any parts which ache.
I shall wish upon a star whether you are near or far.
Pining for a birthday wish. Lamenting at the withheld bliss.
Strolling 'round my local bazaar. How utterly, utterly bizarre.

ONCE UPON A TIME

I sit atop a worn-out bench watching the world go by.
Contemplative. Observant.
The people are dancing in their usual fashion.
Happily chatting away.
Munching on the local delicacies.
Children smoking.
Everything looks the same.
It feels like home.

There's a tranquility in the air.
A peace and happiness I've not felt in quite some time.
It helps to deal with my bewilderment.
I'm still not sure I believe it.
I'm not sure what time it is.
I'm not sure they know what time it is.
I'm not sure if they remember.
I'm not sure if they're real.
But it feels like home.

I feel kind of special.
It was definitely all about me.
I'm sure of that.
I remember the suffering: it can't be forgotten.
That can't be false.

I was chosen.
Picked to take on the forces of darkness.
To be the light that shines through.
To grant freedom to the oppressed.
To teach the world.
Someone has woken me up inside a fairytale.
A fairytale with *smoking* children.

THE MIRROR

I face myself in the mirror as I'm wont to do occasionally.
I see myself for the very first time on every encounter.
Every time I ask, it reflects the same thing.
You are ugly! You are beautiful! You are everything in between!

The person staring back at me looks the same as ever.
This despite my reflection changing each time that I enquire.
Every time I ask, it reflects the same thing.
You are stupid! You're a genius! You are everything in between!

I stare longingly at my reflection hoping my background has changed.
Hoping this time, I see something different. A clue, perhaps?
Every time I ask, it reflects the same thing.
You are a coward! You are brave! You are everything in between!

The ageing man before me is degrading by the day.
The mirror staring back at me has got some games to play.
Every time I ask, it reflects the same thing.
You are imperfect! You're perfect! You are everything in between!

I stand bemused at the person I see staring back at me.
It looks as though only time has changed my humble face.
Every time I ask, it reflects the same thing.
You are worthless! You are valued! You are everything in between!

The mirror stares at me this round as it's wont to do occasionally.
My soul looks different, yet my face remains the same.
This time it asks me, and reflects the same thing:
You are chosen! You're the chosen one! Why do you resist?

ESCAPE INSIDE

A heaped pile upon the floor
My gluttony and laziness are scattered everywhere.
Escape found in every carton.
Every packet.
Every dimp.
Every crumb.
Every stain.

A cathartic release from a world too cruel.
A reality too bemusing.
A set of humans uncharacteristically evil.
Believably, naturally, artfully cold.
Coerced into darkness beyond normality.

The food refrigerates to keep fresh.
The kettle boils, taps running, heat on.
Voices intrude as they will.
Pain suggests as it wants.
The alarm lingers on.

VIPASSANA

Loneliness, has for me, become a state of being.
A place I've visited so often that it is no longer my home.
It is not a place for self-flagellation.
It is no longer merely a place to lament.
It is not simply a place of reflection.
It is not merely a vessel and catalyst for spiritual growth.
It is now a state of being.

Complete oneness with existence.
With its contents and externalities.
With its whims and will.
With its choices and actions.
With its design and designer.
With its vicissitudes and serendipity.
With its eternality and immutability.

RISE

One day we will rise high up in the sky
Where the winds blow strong and the sun shines bright.
In another world where the mind is free.
And the chains that bind us cease to be.

One day we will rise to a higher self.
Where the stars that formed us burn in our hearts.
Like the passing light of a long dead friend.
Guiding us through life from start to end.

One day we will rise to the galaxies above
Through the starlit sky to a nebula.
Until a supermassive black hole sucks us in.
And our new life can at last begin.

One day we will rise to a better being.
Where the love that made us forms anew.
Spreading joy to all who care.
The thoughts of freedom are thus shared.

One day we will rise through the multiverse itself.
In the dying embers of the setting sun.
When the wars are done. When the fight is won.
In another world where the mind is free.
And the chains that bind us cease to be.

TICK-TOCK

Tick-Tock, Tick-Tock clicks the metronomic clock.
Every passing second an unfathomable shock.
An unexpected intruder to a silence sanctified.
An inescapable companion, an army unified.

Tick-Tock, Tick-Tock flows the indefatigable sea.
The stroke of every minute a welcome absentee.
A natural narcissism to a soul sojourn.
A nuanced necromancer to a mind forlorn.

Tick-Tock, Tick-Tock sails the unimpeded ship.
The hand of every hour an alarming trip.
A meticulous invader to a consciousness harried.
Two unrequited lovers begrudgingly are married.

Tick-Tock, Tick-Tock turns the unexpected diary.
The turn of everyday a new line of inquiry.
A suspicious solitude to an unbelieving mind.
Reality and conjecture are thus intertwined.

Tick-Tock, Tick-Tock smoke the mists of mystique.
Every passing week an old and new critique.
An inconspicuous spy to a gullible soul.
Liberty and happiness are living on parole.

Tick-Tock, Tick-Tock chime the bells of time.
Every month renewed an ubiquitous crime.
A never-ending rollercoaster to a sick child.
An enthusiastic sentience forced to be exiled.

DARK MAGIC

I once believed in magic now I see it as a game:
a way to cage the people in this unexplained domain.
What once was used for love has become our biggest stain.
A stain upon humanity wrought by man's selfish aim.
If what we need's a parent to guide us in the dark:
One of fear and jealousy is not the place to start.
A mother of creation is what we all would love
but when I checked the library it said only him above.

The mind demands a journey and just as much a plan.
It will not be denied this not by animal or man.
So then there came the gods and their worshippers to boot.
The shamans casting spells with their knowledge of the flute.
The mind is like an instrument be careful who you trust!
Tricksters lie in ambush so knowledge is a must!
To see into the soul gives us power over all.
The ones who learned this first left us games that still enthrall.

And for every good it does there's nine wrongs that we must bear
for with power comes addiction and addiction is not fair.
The truth was known to them, passed on through generations
then greed became their god and nations our creations.
A way to divide us and keep us at war.
To think our friend is a danger that we should abhor.
They abused all their talents and gifts sent from nature
to create us a world of hardship and labour.

Although you fear the fire and the painfulness of hell,
you really need to think of it as more of a bell
that they tie round your neck and pull on whenever
you must act to accord with their latest endeavour.
I hope I have awakened you with my cautionary words.
The greatest error you can make, blindly following the herd.
For whether sheep or cattle or humans in their droves,
there lies a shepherd in their wake whose motives are untold.

RELIGION

I awoke in an unexplained world with no knowledge of existence
To a world of about eight religions of any significance
Throughout their many cleverly crafted pages
Tell the story of creation and the rules for coexistence

The laws and design of existence is clear in each to see
The designer is ineffable in each of their books
Escape without judgement is not allowed to be
The punishment of doing wrong is in each a guarantee

The rules of life are different in each and each has its own aim
Endless decisions on how to live are made for this domain
The knowledge of start and end is used time and again
The middle passage constructed with a variety of claims

What I took from each was life's a very complex game
Unknowable, unfightable, yet loving just the same
Judgement is the guarantee I pray that God bestows
The only thing within religion I can't say that I know

WAR

You can hear it if you listen closely.
You can watch it as it lands
The shards and remnants of morality
Shattered into a hundred limbs
A thousand bricks
A million tears.
You can smell the innocence
See its red blood splattered on the ground
Taste the sweetness of revenge in the cold air
Hear the joyful cries of children playing
In a park somewhere
Audible over the ubiquitous beating drum of victory
The explosions of supremacy
The gunshots of imperialism.
You can hear them laughing
If you listen closely
As they swing back and forth
Wondering why the sun loves them so much
But the sky seems to hate them
Why it litters their streets with rubble
And massacres their happiness
Are fireworks not for celebrations?
You can see it in your own city
If you care to look
That new railway line that just opened
That trendy new bar you've been wanting to try
Those streets that are always paved
The hospitals that run 24 hours a day.
You can hear the children playing
If you listen closely
If you watch with your eyes
If you think with your mind
But this is an adult's game.
So why are the children playing?

SPECIESISM

The conflict between species is a wondrous sight to see
Their adaptive responses an equilibrated masterpiece
Their intergroup dynamics an ubiquitous decree
The moving reigns of power are forever on lease

The growth of organisms a welcome sage and guide
The constant need for fuel a catalytic aid
The formation of government idiosyncratically supplied
The span of feathered beauty elegantly displayed

The quest to be the ruler an ever-smiling game
Their role within society the overarching objective
The chance to find a mate the ultimate aim
The bonds of friends and family a timeless collective

The competition for survival evolves to status gains
The pursuit for self-provision an unrelenting theme
The attention-seeking actions are without refrain
The bonds of group accomplishment an innovative scheme

The anguished cry of enemies a constant humming howl
The battle for supremacy a timeless, flowing dance
The interaction between lifeforms an intermittent growl
The survival of the species an ever-changing chance

MOO

What do you mean when you say moo?
It's so hard to know because all you say is moo.
Do you think "Well hello there! How do you do?
Wait there a minute, I've got something for you!"
Or do you think that really we ought to shoo?
And that actually people need to eschew
the milk that belongs rightly only to you?
It's so hard to know because you only moo.
You say it so often no matter the view.
Which leaves many options for us to construe.
But what does it feel like - to be you?

Perhaps you feel that we should unscrew
the chains that have bound you hitherto?
That we need to acquire some real virtue
not another dead cow on the barbeque?
Perhaps you feel that we need to review
The methods by which we make you subdue?
Or better yet - to learn to pursue
A meat free option for our life's menu?

Do you mean if it was possible to do
that you'd beat us all with sticks of bamboo?
That you'd kill each of us and our children too?
Then chop us up and make a nice stew
for all the dead cows that we still accrue
some of them killed just for a shoe
to teach us a lesson of how to value
the life of an animal who only says moo.

MEMORIES

It doesn't let me see them anymore.
The memories.
I know it happened.
I remember the screaming.
Always the screams that would wake me up in the middle of the night.
Followed by the sounds of tables being smashed and glass getting cracked.
I remember how he'd cut the telephone wires so we couldn't call the police.
How he'd climb up the side of the house and shout through the open window.
I learnt a lot of words that a nine-year-old should never hear from that 'man'.
I watched a lot of things that no person should watch because of that creature.
I learnt a great many lessons from that psychopath.
Like how to love.
How to treat others.
How to be a good person.
The purpose and value of morality.
What it means to have values. Integrity. Honour.
I still remember the sounds of the windows smashing and the front door being caved in.
I remember the screams of agony from my mother.
I remember him smacking her head off the radiator.
Punching her in the face.
Dragging her around the living room.
But it won't let me see those times anymore.
Just empty rooms, with no sounds and no images and no trauma.
I know I shouldn't, but I've tried to look backwards.
Not because I want to. Not because I need to.
Because, for better or worse, they're part of me.
They helped make me the man I am today.
And I *can* call myself a man.
So, I looked for them.
But they're not there anymore.
It doesn't want me to see them.
It's taken them away from me.
Locked them somewhere so that they can't bother me anymore.
Does it think I'm not strong enough to deal with them?
Or does it just love me so much it couldn't bear to make me watch it a second time?

I don't know.
But I know it happened.
I remember it.

EVIL

Evil is a concept I find hardest to accept.
The desire for suffering most difficult to empathise with.
The enjoyment of injustice the hardest to taste.
The employment of malevolence the strangest choice.

The devil is the concept I find hardest to believe.
That there could be an entity whose entire purpose is evil.
To bring suffering and anguish and fight the tides of good.
Who acts constantly with intentions to deceive.

I couldn't accept this role of any living entity.
Destroying all attempts at good purely out of fun.
The love of wrong I find utterly bemusing.
The devil is an entity I would have to meet personally.

The decision not to play fairly is the easiest to accept.
The desire for self-gratification the humblest of evils.
The enjoyment of enjoyment the most natural choice.
The muting of consequence the sweetest singing voice.

Cruelty is the evil I hate most passionately.
The anguish displayed never causing any empathy.
This I find most perplexing about evil.
I do not understand how it is possible to feel.

EXISTENCE

It seems that I have found myself in a truly insane game.
Precarious is not the word, closer to insane.
The endless possibilities are a wondrous stupefaction.
Their interactivity is a show without cessation.
The juxtaposition from happy times to acts of true terror
Is a violent move of existence I can only deem an error?
How many different forces can be fought at any one time?
The magnitude of reality is beyond sublime.
The variety and complexity that it offers up to see
Is as bewildering as the variety that it offers up to be.
That any given entity could create such a game
Diabolical is not the word, closer to insane.
The fight for good and evil despite its unenforced aim
Is my only reassurance that there is any refrain?
I wonder what the future holds for those who live to see
The smiling face of existence for those it wishes free.
And just as much I'd like to know what it will provide
For those it deems less fortunate and yet here still reside.

THE MIND

The mind is a wonder for all to behold.
Its secrets are many, that you are told.
It learns what it sees from the day that it grows.
Even before then there are things that it knows.

Before there was knowledge spoken by word.
The brain had one mind and through it we learned.
It governs our actions, yet completely confused.
It has all the answers yet still it's bemused.

You ask it a question, the answer it knows.
Then anxiety kicks in and the memory goes.
For when you are anxious the mind never rests.
It's trying to kill you or at least rob your nest.

When we first discovered how to explore our home
The dangers were many with respite unknown.
To keep us all safe it must constantly learn.
All the right answers, some it's never earned.

Despite all the hardship still through it we learn.
What life has to give us and what we should yearn.
With many dead parents who ate the wrong fruit.
And many dead children who were taken by loot.

With hunger and anguish the minds memory grows.
For it will not accept this so to learning it goes.
With blood a conviction it tells us to go.
In whatever direction it thinks we should know.

Yet for every right answer it's learned plenty left.
So, which one to give us to ensure we aren't next?
Despite all this pressure there's more it must do.
That lung isn't working, that limb needs some glue.

DEAR LADIES

Dear ladies! I wrote you a poem so that you all know
That this male thinks that you're all perfect.
To help you appreciate this I decided to show
How women were seen and how they gained respect.

From our very first steps our mothers are there
Ensuring our safety and happiness are protected.
Doting on us simply to let us know that they care.
No reciprocation or reward is ever expected.

They breast feed their children then head out to war.
Reverting to motherhood the instant they return.
Never leaving our sides until they are sure
That we have been given all that we yearn.

Women were the goddesses to which all men once prayed.
From fertility goddesses in the ancient world to Yin and Yang.
Women have been idolised and their delicacy portrayed.
Their femininity and natural features were merrily sang.

Men were obsessed with women and the love they displayed.
Women were the bosom to which they were eternally bound.
Their wisdom and knowledge were keenly conveyed.
Their beauty given licence to perpetually astound.

Their divining skills were fiercely believed.
Their maternalism was irrefutable.
Their compassionate ways were eagerly received.
Their effervescent glow immutable.

The list goes on, so I'll leave it there.
I just wanted to say that I care.

THE SQUARE ROOT OF HAPPINESS

$$Happiness = \left(\frac{Time \times Effort}{Friendship+Family+Activity+Love+Purpose+Spiritual\ Enlightenment}\right)^{Captice}$$

$$Spiritual\ Enlightenment = \left(\frac{Effort}{Purpose}\right)^{Time} - (Friendship + Family + Love + Happiness + Activity + Caprice)$$

$$Family = \left(\frac{Happiness + Love}{Activity + Purpose}\right)^{Time} - (Friendship + Captice + Spiratal\ Enlightment + effort)$$

$$Love = \left(\frac{Happiness}{Friendship+Family+Activity+Purpose}\right)^{Time \times effort \times capirice} - Spiratal\ Enlightment$$

$$Friendship = \left(\frac{Time \times Effort \times Caprice}{Activity + Purpose}\right)^{Love + Happiness} - (Spiritual\ Enlightment + Family)$$

$$Purpose = \left(\frac{Effort}{Friendship+Family+Activity+Love+Happiness+Spiritual\ Enligtenment}\right)^{Time \times Caprice}$$

$$Sqrt\ Happiness = \sqrt[Time \times Effort]{\frac{Caprice}{Friendship \times Family \times Purpose \times Love \times Activity \times Spiritual\ Enlightenment}}$$

AFTERLIFE

Can you just promise me one thing?
That when I die
You'll wake me up and show me.
So that I know once and for all.
That's all I ask.

TRUTH OR DARING?

Did you lie to me?
Or tell me the truth?
I suppose it's a bit like Schrodinger's box.
I both am and am not simultaneously.

LIFE

You can't just go around telling everyone, Nico!
I mean, honestly, what did you expect?

GOODBYE

I didn't realise what you meant
When you told me you loved me.
I never dreamt that you'd be bent
Just to tell me to be free.
I love you too, it should be said
Though our paths have diverged.
Next time rather than use my head
I'd much sooner hear the words.

THANK YOU

Thank you for loving me
when I couldn't love myself.

SMOKING

From the moment that I wake until the moment that I rest.
My lungs are filled with the same poisoned air.
The taste of refined leaf is my only request.
It is my chosen vice; my hourly prayer.

Unjustifiable impurity inhaled without a care.
Freedom and imprisonment intermingle before my eyes.
The stench of tobacco clings to my clothes and hair.
My worries slowly drift up through the skies.

The cries of poverty muted in my mendacious mind.
The pampered pigeon finds a home among the littered streets.
The warnings signs a guide-dog to the willfully blind.
The siren call for playtime plays on repeat.

The unyielding impulse does not cease.
The cathartic release of nicotine an unparalleled clarity.
Still longing for death, yearning for release.
Calling upon my twenty-pack of charity.

MUSIC

Your many soothing recipes flood my ears with joy and time.
Eliciting feelings of glee with every passing rhyme.
The place where I retreat to feel a world away from home.
Escaping into somewhere real; a dancing metronome.
A route to pure catharsis. My ears are full of tears.
A genuine largesse. I could listen for years.

Your mellifluous harmonies are the sweetest dessert.
A double chocolate caramel cake covered in sherbet.
The satisfying salience of melodies renewed.
The voices of angels from within exude.
Cataclysmic symphonies created for the mind.
The place any human can go to unwind.

My heart skips a beat with every passing note.
An epic feat accomplished. Every melody doth gloat.
An anthology of poetry which fills my heart with air.
A nuanced methodology. My welcome daily prayer.
An epic adventure taken with every passing song.
My senses are shaken. My soul, to you, belongs.

FRIENDSHIP

Friendship bright and beautiful I feel you in the sky.
Giving me a sweet embrace and never asking why.
You mean more to be than a thousand empty smiles.
In your love I could spend an eternity exiled.

Friendship beautiful and warm your touch is gracious joy.
I crave your gentle kisses and the love that you employ.
To listen to your dulcet tones causes my heart to cry.
You are to me a million butterflies who made it past the sky.

Friendship glorious and kind, how much I love you.
You brighten up my mind every day that you renew.
The instant you appear happiness is sure to follow.
To know that you are near means never having to be hollow.

"Latch on!" he says to me.
The story of my life.
What friendship's come to be
A battle full of strife.
"Latch on!" I hear reverberating
Around the chambers of my heart.
A life of unremitted waiting
for friendship's flame to start.
"Latch on!" linger his cutting words.
The accuracy unbearable.
It seems he knew my password.
The damage unrepairable.
"Latch on!" his statement penned
of my futile endeavour.
To find myself some friends
other than that girl, Heather.

FAMILY

You don't get to pick your family.
But I'd have picked you all anyway.

LOVE

Love for me has only ever come in one form.
I've never known the feeling of being loved back!
Rejections unrelenting swarm has always showered from above.

I've never shared my life with someone!
And I fear I never will.
The fates have conspired against my happiness.
And given me the bill.

I helped in their endeavor along the way without even noticing.
No matter how my heart strings sway
Reciprocation is a parole hearing!

I wonder what my life will be. And if I'll be loved back.
People could have died for me!
And I'd still feel that I've lacked.

SEX

I enter the room and within five seconds we're already kissing.
Our tongues intertwine as my hands curve the outline of his body.
Reaching down I grab his arse and squeeze.
(God, I hope he's cleaned)

Before long he's on his knees sucking and licking.
I stroke his head for reassurance of a job well done.
Deeper and deeper he takes it.
Having clearly evolved out a gag reflex.
Slowly goes in the first finger to loosen him up.
(God, I hope he's cleaned)

Fingers out and the coast is clear.
Nature has been thwarted.
I slide it in until I hear him moan.
Then I know to slide it out and back in slow.
He moans again as I start to pound.
A familiar scent fills the air.
(But I know he's cleaned)

I carry on until I've cum.
"That was great," he says.
Then goes to clean.
We cuddle in each other's arms.
A parting kiss and then I leave.
(And they say romance is dead)

FLIGHT OF THE STARS

Shining in your eyes I see the stars and their eternal flight.
To look upon you is to find oneself lost within a maze.
A profound familiarity at every single sight.
A single flutter of your eyes leaves me in a daze.
Geometric synchronicity protrudes in every single blink.
The turning tides of fate bestowed an earthly visitation.
The universe and all that's in it daring you to wink.
A reflective light shone with the purest exaltation.
Dancing throughout time and space in an infinite regress.
Extruding a perfection that will forever glow.
Waltzing with majestic grace with unimpeded progress.
Dragging all that is with you wherever you may go.
Flying with the multiverses on their chartered quest.
To find the place at which love's verses find a point of rest.

SPARKLING EYES

The contours of your corpus find a home within my bejewelled eyes.
Your luscious skin stretched tightly, glistening with your entrancing glow.
On each embrace it sends my heart flying formless through the sky.
Answering questions that I thought otherwise impossible to know.
Stark against your sculpted canvas, boldly boasting your splendour.
Hurricanes roar inside my stomach with any godly given glance.
Your every astounding movement absolutely and instantly render.
The fallen fragments of heaven given one timely earthly chance.
Dance for me, my darling, flex your beauty and your mystic might.
Twirl your torso tightly, wind it wantonly within my gleeful gaze.
Stretch and stand still rightly, let me stare in wonder and in awe.
Send me flying head over heels at any encounter and sight.
Leave me speechless as I behold your opulence caught within a haze.
Believe me when I say you're the most beautiful thing that I ever saw.

TAINTED LOVE

To look upon your face is to die a thousand painful deaths.
A soul shaking agony the likes of which hell could not compete.
I'm living in an ocean vainly attempting to catch breaths.
On any encounter my eyes are forced to greet my feet.
Shall I compare thee to a freezing, pitch black night?
The shattered remnants of my heart strewn across the floor.
My cruelly sealed fate despite all of my given might.
The interminable battle for release now a revolving door.
My mind is broken at the mere unwelcome thought.
The devil has claimed a place upon the Earth.
The searing flames of hell have successfully been wrought.
To steal the last remaining dregs of my closely guarded mirth.
The first time I truly met you was the worst day of my life.
Yet still I promise you that you'll never know my strife.

SMILE

Smile a smile that will break my every given defence
Tear down the walls around my barricaded heart
Break into my mind and offer me my recompense
Take me back to the very moment of the very start
One that lights the fires within my beating chest
That renders me useless the instant that you smile
That ensures your love is eternally expressed
And makes me want to sprint the unforgiving mile
A smile that tells me all that I'll ever need to know
That embraces me and warms the fibres of my soul
That comforts me in ways my eyes could never show
And renders me entirely without any self-control
A smile that says what I think a smile should say
That I'll be there for you every minute of the day

SING A SONG FOR ME

Sing a sweet song for me that I may slyly slip to sleep
Close my jaded eyes that I may seek tranquility
Forget my weary troubles and find rest within the deep
Heal my aching wound and shield my vulnerability
Dry my anguished tears to free my tender, tired cheeks
Blow away the fog and make my thoughts completely clear
Release me and take me flying through the starry streaks
Relinquish me to dance away my every given fear
Play a melody for me that will help my soul unwind
Find a note or key that will make it all alright
Rub my blistered back as my soaked bandages unbind
Aid me in my journey on this unchartered flight
Put down my aching heart that it may know its peace
Mute my mourning mind and grant my sweet release

DEAR WORLD

Hidden in your many faces, throughout time and throughout spaces
Within the horrors of the dark, shines a light bright and stark
Illuminating your treasured graces, in your hand replete with aces
Infinity has found its final place, eternal and still without haste.
I see the mirror in your eyes, the lens reflected without lies
Sailing back an endless game, without cause and without blame
Love and hate begin to cry, the grand debate decays and dies
An unforgiven force delayed; an infinite game to be ever played.
Similarities contrast in abstract ways throughout your many nuanced plays
Insanity has found its resting space, an infallible clarity it can't replace.
The clock strides through the day; metered rhythm without delay
Complexity without any restraint; eternity without any complaint.
Smiling through a face of tears, throughout the ever-coming years
Striding boldly without fears shines back a world loved and revered.

THE ETERNAL RIFT

To think about your delicate soul could cause my heart to die
You are beyond the love of all, beyond all other sacrifice
The suffering tolled for your compassion causes my mind to cry
The fates of folly and of fortune play with their willing dice
An Angel fell upon the Earth to bring good to all those good
Rejoiced and all resolving, loving through the horror and pain
Taking vengeance at the wicked, slayed them as you knew you should
Recompense and restitution are now flowing without any refrain
The light you brought to those who need it: I can only begin to hope
Is in some way compensation for your needlessly suffered soul
A sacrifice beyond forgiveness, given freely as a gallant gift
Now you have been tested and rested, now you can freely elope
Your beautiful heart and your valorous virtue can again be extolled
Plugging the cosmic fabric with the force to fill its once eternal rift

SPACE AND TIME

Floating in your opaque ocean led adrift through stunning summer streams
Secure within your tangled web of beauty and all that it calls calmly near
Swimming vainly in your embrace through your many thoughts and dreams
Brightening up the air around to make the viewpoint all the more clear
Rendered feeble at the thought of ever even contemplating letting go
Paralyzed upon the act of placing power in so saintly and delicate of hands
Talking all the tales that one life could possibly portent or show
Patiently falling through the grains of time's methodically poured sands
Lounging lightly in the layered rays and all the goodness that it can provide
Protection and comfort intertwine, a lesson learned there to remind
The questions answered through the waves that will forever reside
Upon the shores of space and time as it untethers and unbinds
Willing you to ask the questions that you know you need to ask
Choosing the right answer to use, is, I find, the hardest of the tasks

FORTUNE

Serendipity you are the beams of sunshine in the sky
Fallen upon the ground at the most fortuitous of hours
Your delights are derived without ever asking why
A beautiful butterfly upon the most delicate of flowers
Vicissitude you pouncing tiger in the darkened night
Swooped upon your prey at the most fortuitous of times
Your unsuspecting attack announced without any sight
The spider casts its steady web and patiently climbs
Caprice you cunning cuttlefish within the temperate sea
Freely swimming within the dark and daring ocean
Your circumstances leave many alternatives to be
A newly found and mysterious bottled magic potion
Call to me all three of you, come together and unite
Guide my life within your knowing vision and sight

MUSE

Muse your mystic wonderings into my consolidating deductions
      Reveal your secrets to my acquiescent, inquisitive, inquiring mind
Tell me all that there is to know, all that I may discover and find
      Move all that has and will be into the most simplified of reductions
Wow me with your enigmatic, ingenuous, ruminations and revelations
      Disambiguate my deluded definitions of all I've ever known to be
Aid my mind in its endeavour to more coherently and correctly see
      Illuminate the path that you laid, grown firm from your foundations
Disabuse my calculations and determinations of this bewildering world
      Speak you spell of superlatives to my disbelieving yet yearning soul
Take my disorganised, denying mind for its welcomed, wondering stroll
      Leave my consciousness in disarray as my thoughts are forced to whirl
Sooth my soul with speculations, every day some newfound conjecture
      Within resides a craving consciousness for any and all of your lectures

TEARS

Glistening in the tear that trickles gently down your cheek
Glimmers the knowledge, wisdom and secrets of your soul
It says something familiar and yet says something unique
I wouldn't waste its value with any attempts to console
It tells me all that I can read as I gaze upon your face
It speaks from your soul saying what I need to know
Obviating your many attributes to light up your grace
Your soul seeped out through your eyes to cries of wow
Falling upon the ground with the finality of fate
Calling to an end the eternal, internal discussions
Every passing tear does yet more beauty create
The droplets and rivulets filled with repercussions
From a soul that is full of all the necessary feelings
To bring about recompense, restitution and healing

NAIVETÉ

Naiveté, my dear sweet child, what is there that could be said?
I told you once, I told you twice, I told you two times more.
Foolishness, daughter of mine, what happens within your head?
I guess that now you've played your cards, you're finally sure.
To fathom what is so unfathomable to you as you simply think.
And stumble at every hurdle, at every marked, signposted path.
Dumfounded and flabbergasted have been used to their brink.
A part of my soul wants to wail; my head tells me to simply laugh.
Gullibility, dear daughter, it seems it's possible for you to disbelieve.
To stare straight into my eyes and fail to clearly see the reflection.
My soul called out for yours in hopes that you would believe.
That you'd take my hand so that I might offer you my protection.
Naiveté, my dearest darling, all that I have left to do is to hope:
That time will hear your screaming wounds and offer you the rope.

REVULSION

The churning of my stomach every time that I see your face
The vomit upon my throat each time I recall your name
The sickness in my mind with each attempt at an embrace
The bewilderment I feel to think of my unrequited fame
The fury I feel at the mere thought of every life you've harmed
The frustration that burns every time I see you not in pain
The irascibility of my soul as I see the world you've farmed
The itchiness I feel every time I see you that irritates my brain
The bulging in my veins as I contemplate your nuanced hate
The anguish bubbling in my soul at every stolen treasure
The apoplectic rage as you justify your sickness as natural fate
The revulsion as you consume your every greedy pleasure
The anxiety running through my gut as I recall your face
And how it used to look to me: not remotely out of place

A PART OF YOU

On each encounter I have with your silhouette
Every memory that it breeds and each regret
The lamentation that I feel and confliction I get
There's still a part of me that refuses to forget
I cannot but think of you without wanting to cry
And simultaneously hope that each of you die
As I relentlessly and vainly attempt to try
To find what good there is within the goodbye
And while you will never look the same again
My forgiveness impossible for you to ascertain
A friendship and trust that you'll never regain
The Polaroids I have of you will always remain
Thus, when I look upon you I can still believe
There is still a part of you that refused to leave

VICE AND VIRTUE

Vice and virtue are to me a sort of eternal Yin and Yang
A tango team that must both exist together to perform
The catalyst from which my hopes and dreams have sprang
Offering up wisdom, guidance, knowledge and reform
They play together as two children skipping ropes
Jumping up and down together, hand in hand
The place where I place all of my dreams and hopes
And watch them shatter on the ground as they land
The dedicated duo; never have been seen apart
Where one is found the other is sure to be
Virtue could not be known without its counterpart
Vice is the vehicle by which it becomes free
Vice and virtue are to me a sort of father and mother
Without one there simply cannot be the other

SORRY

Sorry I was not fully the human that I wished that I could be
Unable to provide for you an easily esteemed representative
That I was not the example setter I wanted you all to see
That the best I could offer up was to be argumentative
Sorry that I chose some things I regret having chosen
For anyone I've hurt as I've grown up within this world
To any innocent who my many words may have frozen
Anything that I said wrong in haste as my reality whirled
Sorry for the actions I've taken that I myself regret
For every failure I embodied as I fought the good fight
For every gluttonous indulgence and every unpaid debt
For every drooping layer of fat that will forever be in sight
Sorry that I was not able to be the person that I see
When I look at myself in my mind and yearn to be free.

RICO

My name is fucking Nico! I find myself screaming at hospital staff
Not Rico, traitor, or devil, nor any other title you might like to add.
I don't expect to see your spite as I try to run my bubble bath
I'm the second fucking coming bitch, not some flying fucking fad!
My name's not fucking Rico! Go and learn some damned respect!
You're all glorified administrators riding others' coattail winds.
Just do your fucking job and find freshly pressed linen to select.
Don't interrupt my sanity with your delusions that I sinned.
My name is fucking Nico! I scream for the last fucking attempt.
The multi-pronged assault too much for my delicate soul to bear.
It seems that as fair treatment goes, I have found myself exempt.
A willful misuse of my name it seems is all that they can share.
My name's not fucking Rico! I scream with the entirety of my soul.
I spit upon their pitiful attempts to destroy my self-control.

PERSECUTION

I cannot begin to tell you how pathetic that you are.
How disgusting I find you, and how equally bizarre.
That you would irritate and hurt me as I write the world a gift
With some attack or impediment no matter the time of shift.
It shakes me to my very core to think of what you'll do
To oppress me and anyone with progression to pursue.
That you would hinder all attempts to rise with a thought trial
While smiling with that sickening disingenuous fucking smile
That somehow manages to reach the corner of your eyes
Not once displaying anywhere the extent of your lies
It makes me want to harm you in ways I'd otherwise deem crude
Had I not met a group of people so *unbelievably fucking rude.*
To viciously brutalize and threaten me within the open air
To enslave me within my mind and boast that you don't care
To rifle through my every thought and consider it a crime
Whilst hurting me and framing me all at the one time.
To project racial abuse, slavery and brazen open hate
Into my loving mind as some kind of fucking speech or debate.
To then assault me further as you flogged me through the streets
With no concern from any person I was misfortunate enough to meet.
I cannot begin to express to you the hatred that I now hold.
The ways I'd make you all suffer are simply best left untold.

OPPRESSION

Oppression is a cruel reality I'm sad to say I know
Mistreatment from the start of life and all throughout the show
Hidden behind smiles that I thought would forever glow
Resided a true monster that I got to know too slow

Perniciously harassing me and harming my soft heart
The ugly tides of time have caused my love to depart
Harassment in my mind as a crime for being smart
Denying me the right to freely create my art

Every given gesture was designed to one day hurt
All of my thoughts and actions scripted to help subvert
My every waking day I'm living on high alert
Reduced to feeling helplessly inert

The people that I thought that I once knew
Became a group I wish I personally slew
Several rights that are infallible they apparently withdrew
The ties of friendship can never renew

The anguish in my brain every coming day
Is more than I can bare without having to say
That I hate existence just as much as any of its prey
Still, here I sit writing in the present day

SUICIDE

I've been driven to thoughts of suicide by a society I called home
The majority of its people a callous, wicked group of fiends
They enslaved me on hate-vision and told me to kill myself
Rewarding me with empty cities free to roam

The people here are evil, the vilest of the vile
What once was a community is now a place of exile
The bodies layer up, pile upon pile
Still hatred is ready to drive the extra, unforgiving mile

I wonder what their ancestors would think about the game
Having harmed innocents historically without a care
The extra added boastfulness of unabashed cruelty
Is an unbecoming reality which they too easily became

To stay in this world with every evil act
Would be to call the devil for a friendly pact
I will not live with people who only display tact
My approval of their humanity I heartily retract

I will say this here in case I choose to die
That this world is to me nothing more than a lie
Take my angry poem as my only goodbye
I do not wish to see any of you if I make it past the sky

RAGE

My stomach boils and my arms shake
The pounding of my heart reverberates through my shaking soul
Reality weighs down its crushing cry
My soul threatens to break

                Upon a land I once called home resided a true evil
                   Cruelty and detachment without a current equal
              I look upon their lying face with unparalleled anger
                      No action I could take would satiate my rage

Sociopathy is not a trait that I admire in humans
I couldn't look them in the eye without wanting to kill them
Every time I think about it my body fills with rage
There isn't enough suffering as I fill up my page

              Would fate and justice be so kind as to rectify the wrong
                Will it ever scold the hind of this unfeeling throng?
                  The answered cry of innocence leaves me apoplectic
                        I'll never know peace until they suffer

I scream in my head every day as I reflect
There isn't a pitch high enough for them to scream
My mind has to resort to denial just to cope
For every child this community failed to protect

              My anguished, clenched fists are raised ready to fight
              The anguished cry of children the display of their might
                  And as I observe their sickening justifications
                      It only acts to lower them in my estimations

To look upon a screaming child and then attack
Is more than my soul can endure without wanting revenge
And as if sickness couldn't find a home better suited to its needs
They glorify their murderers and adorn them as a plaque

            There isn't a word I could write that would express my rage
                  No melody or rhyme that could cause it to abate
              For every child that they harmed as a result of their hate
            I hope they burn one thousand-fold, and still I'll be enraged

TEARS II

My eyes are filling up with tears though I am not allowed to cry.
It is something denied to me by which ever powers be.
My aching heart pangs the same, constantly assigning blame.
Reminding me of all the pain; the memories will not refrain.
The injustice is too hard to bear: too many people did not care.
Each attack still lingers on from the day the fight was won.
I can't accept what they did to me even though I was set free.
They had no right to mistreat me! Though it only brought them glee.
What has happened to my world? Reality has now been blurred.
It couldn't happen in my home not merely for a throne.
No society could partake in such barbarity for evil's sake.
They broke every trust I gave in their quest to make me a slave.
A truly sickening assault yet I'm the only one at fault.
My screaming soul cannot be satiated until I hear them scream!
My loving heart is fully crushed, my fighting spirit duly hushed.
It's more than anyone could bear to be pinned down as the wolves tear.
My soul is weeping every day, it cannot be kept at bay.
And all that's showing in my eyes is the driest of lies.

WHY ARE YOU *LIKE* ATTACING MARKETING

Why are you *like* attacking marketing? The daft bitch says to me.
Because I have a soul, I think? Because I wish to live life free?
Without the burning knowledge of the most important recent thing
Or what exceptional untold joys the purchase is supposed to bring.
That as I meander down the street and ponder this provincial palace
I am without the injected impulse to buy the latest golden chalice.
That I may discover life's mysteries and quench my edacious mind
With the knowledge of just *anything* else that it is able to find.
Because, my dear, within my mind I reserve a special place
For the vital mental processes that it endeavours to replace.
So that when I awake in the morning or lay my head to rest
I have not one vision, sound or memory with which to wrest.

Why are you *like* attacking marketing? The bimbo boldly states.
Sitting still and looking pretty, a walking marketing update.
The fat swiftly licked from his greedy, self-indulgent lips;
His many meaningless mutterings and worthless shopping trips.
Because, my dear, despite your *irrefutably* attractive and fair face
There's more of you to interpret that your looks do little to efface.
Thus, when I seek to render you and your every given compulsion
I am at once overcome by an immutable feeling of revulsion.
That when I look upon your face and your soulless, seeing eyes
There is just one thing I see that I do not vehemently despise.
So that if ever you should look upon yourself and seek to see:
You might find within yourself a slave I have set free.

DEAD SYRIAN REFUGEES

Dead Syrian refugees, he says
And *smiles*, and *flirts* and *gayly* waves
A bloated seal among the knaves
His treasure trove inhaled by nose
The childish air of spoilt sperm
The griddled fat, the red plump worm
Unprecedented bile of a new firm
The children's cries once more impose

Dead Syrian refugees, he says
And boasts of shags and how he lays
A can by hand, a spliff by choice
A short remark of singing voice
A chatter here, a chatter there
A little stroke, a half-arsed care
A meaningful life full of purpose
To live off bread and dance circus

SMILING LIES

> Everything I've ever known
> Is now to me a lie
> Every kindness I've experienced
> Has caused my soul to die

The deceit and lies are endless
No truth was ever told
Every 'human' I've ever met
Was a lie willfully sold

> I would not have thought it possible
> That people could be so cruel
> To make up to be a victim
> A child still at school

The place within their hearts
That should be filled by love
Was artfully manipulated
From orders up above

> All I really have to say
> Is that I'm lost for words
> The second time in existence
> That my speech is slurred

SCUM

All I have to say to each one of you worthless fucking scum
Is go and fucking boil yourself and repeat when you're done
And if you should ever find your suffering comes to an end
Find another way to harm yourself and all your vile friends

ENOUGH

I just need to let you know here and now it'll never be enough!
No action can now be taken! No retribution too rough!
The sickness I feel every time I recall what you are:
To not induce within you shame: I can only find bizarre!

BRITISH CHARM

Just who the fuck do you people think that you fucking are?
To brutalize, to tyrannize, to threaten, and then to hide the scars.
The cowardice, the cruelty and sheer superfluous fucking harm!
I can only assume, is what I've heard, of famous British charm?

NIGGER

Nigger he says to me within a home I helped to build.
A shelter from his own damn greed, the price of help fulfilled.
Shot from his tongue, his weaponry, at face-blank range.
It felt new, it felt old, it felt wrong, it felt strange.

FEAR

I really must say that you all appear remarkably fucking calm!
I get the urge to run away every time I think about the alarm.
That any dial could go so senselessly high for units such as pain
It leaves me speechless every time I see people in this domain.

HUNTING

The sheer magnitude of variety displayed neatly for me to see
is more than my soul can endure without in some way getting poor.
I think I spend more time looking for things to do when I'm cooking
than I would spend out in the wild. Utopia lives in this aisle.

FACES

To which of your faces should I respond?
And what reply to play?
I'm not sure what would correspond.
Or what to really say.

BETRAYAL

A burning knife within the slots of my fragile bones.
A broken heart, a naïve love, a wrongly trusted friend.
A gluttonous group of hypocrites freely throwing stones.
An agony the likes of which little else could contend.

FORCE

A spider standing brazen without fear in the face of certain end
A housewife with makeup to wear and broken bones to mend
A shooting star, a swirling world, an exploding galaxy
A laser aimed inside my head as I refuse to be unfree

R.E.S.P.E.C.T.

If I meet one more person who denies me respect where it is due
I feel that I may well explode, take out a gun and then reload.
I cannot bear to live like this, to be harmed without witness
To then meander down the street with yet more hurdles to defeat.
The multi-pronged mental assault for someone clearly not at fault
Is more than I can truly bear without wondering just how they dare.
The bloodied mind, the subtle slice, the victory dance cannot suffice.
They want to let me know: my harm can fund their worthless show.

DIES IRAE

Once upon an evening placid, while conversing, soaked in acid,
Over many a quaint and curious volume of forgotten lore—
While I answered, often screaming, suddenly there came a dreaming,
As of someone deftly scheming, scheming for the end of war.
"'Tis some visitor," they mocked, "some unholy guarantor."
Only this and nothing more.

Ah, distinctly I remember, it was in the bleak December;
And each separate dying ember wrought its ghost upon my skin.
Eagerly I wished for freedom; —as I vainly sought to free them
From the tenterhooks of slavery —bravery at the battle within.
From the evil, tyrant Jezebel whom the devil named Elizabeth.
Nameless *here* for evermore.

And the assured, enforced drinking of each purple, poisoned drink
Thrilled me —filled me with fantastic terrors never felt before;
So that now, to still my heart's beating, I sat angrily repeating
"'Tis some unjust justice entreating entrance at my psyche's door!
Some unjust justice entreating entrance at my psyche's door!"
This it is and nothing more.

Presently my soul grew stronger; hesitating then no longer,
"Madam," said I, "or fiend, truly your righteousness I implore!"
But the fact is they kept hacking, and so eagerly attacking,
And so brashly they came smacking, smacking at my chambered soul.
That I scarce was sure I heard her —here I gave her full control;
Lightness there and nothing more.

Deep into that darkness peering, long I sat there wondering, fearing,
Doubting, dreaming dreams no mortal ever dared to dream before.
But the assault was unbroken, and the anguish gave no token,
And the only word there spoken was the whispered word, "Lenore?"
This I whispered, and an echo murmured back the word, "Lenore!"
Merely this and nothing more.

Immobilised, my stomach churning, all my soul within me burning,
Soon again they came attacking somewhat harsher than before.
"Surely," said I, "that is something that cannot be done in law!"
Let me see, then, what thereat is, and this mystery explore.
Let my heart be still one moment and this mystery explore.

'Tis the wind and nothing more!

Open then flung my mind's shutter, when, with many a slurred stutter,
In there swooped a state-owned vulture of the demonic days of yore.
Not the least obeisance made she; just one second paused or swayed she
And, with mien of imp and lackey, entreated entrance at my psyche's door.
Perched upon a lattice, laughing, prized entrance to my psyche's door.
Scathed, and spat, and nothing more!

Then this ivory vulture unsmiling, carried on my crimes compiling
By the grave and stern impropriety of the power that she bore.
"Though thy face be shorn and shaven, thou," I said, "art sure no haven.
Ghastly, grim and modern craven, bloated from the loots galore!
Tell me what thy wicked aim is forcing entrance to my psyche's door!"
Quoth the craven, "Evermore."

Much I marveled this ungainly fowl to hear evil so plainly howl.
Still I answered her with integrity —with little efficacy wrought;
Yet I cannot help agreeing that no living human being
Ever yet was blessed with seeing what displayed at my psyche's door:
Perfection, peace and purity projected from my psyche's door.
Named *here* forevermore.

But the vulture, sitting solely on the latticed chair, spoke only
Those two words, as if her soul in those two words it outpoured.
Every scathing word she uttered —every insult that she muttered
Till I scarcely more than spluttered, "I will be heard upon the board!"
Still their onslaught was unceasing, the barbarism still increasing.
Then spoke the demon, "Evermore."

Startled at the evil spoken, my reply so aptly broken;
"Doubtless," said I, "what it utters is its only stock and store."
Caught from some unhappy master, some unmerciful disaster;
Followed fast and followed faster with the burdens that I bore—
Till the dregs of my ransacked soul lay lamenting, broken and sore.
Spoke the demon, "Evermore!"

But the vulture still unsmiling, carried on my crimes compiling,
Some unwelcome visitor forcing entrance to my psyche's door;
Then, upon the empire sinking, thoughts of freedom interlinking
Fancy unto fancy, thinking what this ominous banshee of yore—
What this grim, ungainly, ghastly, gaunt, and ominous banshee of yore.
Meant in wailing, "Nevermore."

Thus, I sat engaged in guessing, with cries of pain expressing
To the fowl whose fiery eyes now burned into my soul's core;
This and more I sat divining, the rights of humans defining,
Caught within the fiery, foul clasps of the satanic cult of England.
By the vile, venomous, vicious, viperous, vulgar, satanic cult of England.
She shall press, ah, nevermore!

Then, I felt the air grow hotter, framed as a Guy Fawkes plotter,
As someone plainly scheming, dreaming for the end of war.
"Wretch," I cried, "thy God hath lent thee —by the devil he hath sent thee.
Repent! Repent! Wicked banshee from thy memories of before.
Repent! Repent! Demonic hounds from thine iniquities galore."
Only this and nothing more.

"Prophet?" said I, "thing of evil! —Evil still, if queen or peasant!"
Whether tempter sent, or whether tempest tossed thee here ashore.
Undesolate yet all desiring, on this forgotten land expiring,
On this home of horrors conspiring —tell me, truly, I implore!
Is there —*Is* there any chance of redemption? Tell me, tell me, I implore!
Quoth the demon, "Evermore."

"Prophet!" said I, "thing of good! —Prophet still, if framed or harmed!"
By that Heaven that bends around us —by that God you claim to adore.
To this soul whose aid you encumbered, still with accolades outnumbered.
It has passed a foreboded, fated prophet whom the angels named Nico.
It has passed a rare and radiant prophet whom the angels named Nico.
Named here forevermore.

"Be that word our sign of parting, vile fiend!" I shrieked, upstarting.
"Get thee back into the tempest, abate your sickening attack!
Leave no white plume as a token of the lies thy souls hath spoken!
Leave my happiness unbroken! Quit the bust above my door!
Take thy claws from out my heart and take thy foot from off my back!"
Spat the devil, "Nevermore."

And the fiends, never flitting, still are sitting, *still* are sitting.
Tapping, rapping, keenly attacking the pureness of my soul.
And their eyes have all the seeming of a demon's that is dreaming,
And the lamplight over streaming throws their shadow on the floor;
And my soul from out that darkness that lies golden evermore.
Shall be golden forevermore!

A PLEASING NOD

On a tepid, calm December day
The fates of hell were kept at bay.
A monumental gauntlet thrown
To usurp those who use a throne.

Questions! Accusations! Lies!
Answers never heard.
Abuse! Degrade! Despise!
A defence with all words slurred.

A cunning, spiteful, evil witch
Did before God attempt to bitch.
Hiding in her concrete towers
Before God she rightly cowers.

Destroy! Pervert! Incriminate!
Parried with a lofty flick.
Attack! Abate! Obliterate!
Ok, then! A lunatic!

Then for him to hear his name.
Acquainted only with his shame.
Brought tears before the eyes of God,
A quiet, gentle, pleasing nod.

MARCHING ORDERS

I find myself within a cage that's not supposed to exist
An added layer to reality I feel I must resist
And every time I wonder how it all could be
I open up my eyes and all too clearly see
The madness that lies behind me is just as clear ahead
The road lays worn, sodden and roughly tread
The vulture swoops to prey it doesn't need to eat
And boasts of its compassion as it lays bloody in defeat
The screaming wind of innocence vainly attempts to howl
Rendered useless against the pack's militarized growl
The siren song of pride and prejudice has reached melodies malign
The added pitch of cruelty an unfathomable design
So, ahead lies the burden that seems the greatest weight they bear
That in the game of existence there is the concept fair!
That just as much I've heard of concepts, good, and right, and just
And I have in my knowledge the words kind, righteous and trust
And on my short, wondering travels I've met more words as well
That make my heart strings flow and anxiety swell
So, again I look upon the Earth with newly seeing eyes
With tales to tell and new perspectives to advise
To you, I say, go boldly where no human has before gone
And work the cogs of justice once you arrive thereupon
Toiling day and night until you meet your faultless end
The mighty rod of righteousness, go gallantly defend!
And when your aching muscles have cried their last tired tear
Redouble all your efforts for the next ten coming years
Seek out injustice and pluck it by its heinous horns
For you it will be looking, impeded only as it self-adorns
Smite it as the wicked fiend that in life it chose to be
Defend those that it relentlessly captivates unfree
Relinquish from the hand of evil all that it holds dear
And cleave it swiftly off; without guilt and without fear
Look upon the needy, the wicked and the damned
And feed them all with the same unflinching hand
And when they disregard your gift and yet still ask for more
Know what it is that you knew the day before
Go! Valiantly! Fight for the benefit of what you know is right
No matter the day or time that you find malevolence in flight
Only with your perpetual fight against the dark
Will the lending ear of humanity begin to hark!

I'M NOT YOUR SLAVE

How many different ways can I find to help convey:
I'm not your slave, not yesterday, tomorrow or today
I didn't ask, I did not tell, I didn't plead, I did not yell
I said: I'm not your slave! I choose to choose, to misbehave

You beat me within the air without concern or any care
Still, I fight on despite the hate; I will endeavour to be great
To walk about with a straight back; never caring to look back
Your words will never break me: I am and always will be free

No matter what life throws my way, I will succeed every day
I'll still endeavour to achieve each dream that I conceive
I am the wind at gale force: I am the underlying source
My mind is mine alone, where I reside, and I alone own

Try as you might to be my better, my words will break your fetters
The manacles are swiftly cast aside; no more within shall I reside
My soul is pure, my mind is true. Let liberty run where it's due:
I'm not your slave! I'll never be! How dare you ask a man like me?!

DEAR MOTHER AFRICA

Dear Mother Africa, why are you beset with gloom?
Have all of your happy memories been taken?
Do you not remember the Sudanese and their tombs?
The fighting spirit and victory of the Haitians?

Have you forgotten the Garden of Eden?
The stretched all the way down to Abyssinia.
When you built Courts of Law to make things even?
Do you not recall our role on Pangea?

Do the people of the Zanj mean nothing to you?
Has Mansa Musa slipped your loving mind?
What about our mathematical breakthroughs?
Remember! Remember! The birth of mankind.

Oh, Mother Africa, how much you've endured.
What things you've achieved, how much you have learned.
Believe! Believe! The future is yours!
What has been stolen can yet be returned!

Does the long walk to freedom not fill you with hope?
Do you not see the kings you have crowned?
Do you not see the elephants, the free antelope?
Remember! Remember! You once were renowned.

Can you not fathom the laws you have shaped?
Do you not recall the might of your power?
Don't you realise what you've given Earth's Apes?
Carpe Diem! Think! This is our golden hour!

Dear Mother Africa, is that a smile on your face?
Have you recalled all that was? All that can be?
Have you learned once more to have pride in your race?
Do you finally believe once again you'll be free?

THE GOOD MAN'S BURDEN

Take up the Good Man's burden—
   Send forth the best ye breed—
Release your daughters from exile
   To serve your captive needs.
Go! Fight in heavy armour
   For freedom, folk and child.
Set free the oppressed peoples,
   Let righteousness run wild.

Take up the Good Man's burden—
   In patience to abide,
To veil the threat of terror
   And check the show of pride;
By open speech and simple,
   An hundred times made plain.
To seek another's profit,
   And work another's gain.

Take up the Good Man's burden—
   The savage wars of peace—
Fill full the mouth of Famine
   And bid the sickness cease;
And when your goal is nearest
   The end of others fought,
Watch work and virtue, rightly
   Bring all the dreams you sought.

Take up the Good Man's burden—
   No tawdry rule of kings,
But toil of serf and sweeper—
   The tale of common things.
The ports ye shall now enter,
   The roads ye shall now tread,
Go make them with your living,
   And mark them with your dead!

Take up the Good Man's burden—
   And reap his old reward:
The guard of those ye blame,
   The love of those ye hate—

The cry of hosts ye humour
   (Ah, slowly!) toward the light:—
"Why brought ye us from bondage,
   Our half-loved, half-Negro knight?"

Take up the Good Man's burden—
   Ye dare not stoop to less—
Nor call too loud on Freedom
   To cloak your weariness;
By all ye cry or whisper,
   By all ye leave or do,
The silent, sullen peoples
   Have weighed your Gods and you.

Take up the Good Man's burden—
   Have done with devilish ways—
The lightly proffered laurel,
   The easy, ungrudged praise.
Come now, to search your manhood
   Through all the thankless years,
Cold-edged with dear-bought wisdom,
   The judgment of your peers!

I DID NOT STAND AT YOUR GRAVE AND CRY

I did not stand at your grave and cry.
I did not even attempt to try.
I did not stand at your grave and weep.
Though I sincerely hope you sleep.
I wish you all that death can bring.
For you I hope the angels sing.
On bended knee upon the clouds
The day that they remove your shroud.
I did not stand at your grave and cry.
I did not wish to tell a lie.
I did not stand at your grave and weep.
I wished you rest within the deep.
I hope you fly through time and space.
A fate befitting your love and grace.
I hope that now you are released
You will know everlasting peace.
I pray that God accepts your soul
And takes you for a welcome stroll.
Plays a symphony for you
The moment you are welcomed through.
Holds you in a warm embrace
Your consciousness fully encased.
Answers your many questions
Offering up new suggestions.
I did not stand at your grave and cry.
I bought you all that love can buy.
I wished for you infinite things
With more joy than each one could bring.
I hope you know all that can be learned.
Experiencing all that can be yearned.
That you will enjoy your new life
Never knowing any strife.
Meet with those you love once more
Chatting on your favourite shore.
The winds of happiness blowing.
The tides of reflection flowing.
I did not stand at your grave and cry.
I did not ever question why.
I did not stand at your grave and weep.
Your memories I chose to keep.

I hope you feel in love forever
Frolicking with whomsoever.
Experiencing all that love can proffer.
Taken aback at every offer.
That you will have ten thousand friends
With conversations that never end.
Flying through the universe
The moment that you leave your hearse.
I did not stand at your grave and weep
I left your soul for God to reap.
I did not stand at your grave and cry.
I wished for you to sail the sky.
I hope you swim an endless sea
And grow into a mighty tree.
I hope the heavens fall in love
And crash to Earth from up above.
That you will know tranquility
To match your affability.
A happiness without restraint.
An eternity without complaint.
I did not stand at your grave and weep.
You are not there; you do not sleep.
I did not stand at your grave and cry.
You are not there; you did not die.

THE PRAYER

Our Creator, who art heaven, hallowed is thy name.
Thy faithdom come, thy will be done, on Earth as it is in Heaven.
I vow to thee my God, all heavenly things above:
Entire, and whole, and perfect, the service of my love.
The faith that asks no questions, the pride that pays the price:
The bond that makes undaunted the final sacrifice.
A parent and a friend: A guide within this test;
That lays upon your alter our dearest and our best.
Lead us not into temptation and inspire within us good.
Deliver us from evil to cement our righteous neighborhood.
Forgive us our trespasses as we forgive those few
Who choose within their hearts another path than you.
We may not count your armies yet see the good you bring.
Our fortress is a faithful heart; our pride is suffering.
And soul by soul and silently your shining bounds increase.
Your ways are ways of gentleness and all your paths are peace.

GOD RISES

A Phoenix ascending from the embers of its own flesh.
Wings spread in anticipation of flight.
Launched elegantly into action.
G O D R I S E S

A stampede vibrating the sturdy ground beneath it.
The caprice of nature harmoniously equilibrating.
In an eternal improvisation.
G O D R I S E S

A Butterfly tearing through its cocoon.
The shards of its once beloved home discarded.
Patiently waiting to morph into something new.
G O D R I S E S

A solar hurricane coalescing everything in its path.
Fragments of elements cascading space.
Forced into new structures.
G O D R I S E S

A Lotus valiantly breaking through the murky swamp.
Its delicate petals stretched to reach the light.
Defiantly contesting its drowned lungs.
G O D R I S E S

An orchestra composing music as it performs.
The tendrils of harmony secured firmly to the melody.
The rhythm in constant crescendo.
G O D R I S E S

An Eagle swooping from the skies to its dinner.
The prey caught between its claws.
Vainly attempting to escape.
G O D R I S E S

A NOTE FROM THE AUTHOR

Thank you for taking the time to read my diary. I hope you found as much enjoyment reading it as I found catharsis in writing it.

The anthology was written within a period of psychosis, during the Carona Virus pandemic, at which time I believed I had been subjected to a horrific duress interview with the British Intelligence Services. And while I vacillate between belief and disbelief on this, given the very vivid memories I have of the occurrence, what I now know is that none of you watched it. All the jeers I heard were created by a computer (or my brain – if you prefer to believe so), and all the things I thought you had done as a society were simply not true.

And so, I want you to know that most of the sentiments expressed in pages 68-88 are not necessarily my views anymore, but I felt they should be maintained in the anthology as they were indeed my thoughts and feelings at the time.

This is my home. I know that now.

With love,
Nico.

ACKNOWLEDGEMENT

This anthology depicts reworkings of the following poems:

1. The Raven - Edgar Allen Poe
2. The white man's burden - Rudyard Kipling
3. Do not stand at my grave and weep - Clare Harner
4. I vow to thee my country - Cecil Spring Rice
5. The Lord's Prayer - Saint Matthew

www.ingramcontent.com/pod-product-compliance
Lightning Source LLC
Chambersburg PA
CBHW021117080526
44587CB00010B/551